THE
AUTHENTIC
AMERICAN
JOHNBOAT

THE AUTHENTIC AMERICAN JOHNBOAT

How to Build It, How to Use It

LARRY DABLEMONT

Drawings by Bob Martin
Photos by Larry Dablemont

David McKay Company, Inc.
New York

Library of Congress Cataloging in Publication Data

Dablemont, Larry.
  The authentic American johnboat.

  Includes index.
  1. Johnboats.   I. Title.
VM351.D23   623.82′9   78-6528
ISBN 0-679-50861-9

1 2 3 4 5 6 7 8 9 10

Manufactured in the United States of America

Design by Remo R. Duchi

Contents

Chapter 1

Growing Up
with Johnboats

As far back as I can remember, we always had johnboats in our back yard. They sat on sawhorses beneath the big elm tree, 2 or 3 at a time.

Dad would rent them on weekends during the spring and summer. And occasionally the folks who floated the rivers of the Ozarks would ask him to build one.

That was in the late 1950's and early 1960's. In those days it seemed that most rivers had 2 or 3 wooden johnboats chained and locked to trees at every access point.

These wooden boats played a big part in the lives of river families across the nation for several decades, but I don't suppose they meant more to anyone than they meant to the Dablemonts.

My grandfather, Fred Dablemont, was 10 years old just after the turn of the century and it was then that he first saw the Ozarks of south-central Missouri. The Big Piney River flowed into the Gasconade just a few miles from the farm his father (my great-grandfather) bought. As a boy, my grandfather was quick to acquaint himself with the flocks of wild turkey that roosted along the river and with the flocks of waterfowl that dropped in to feed along the Big Piney in the fall.

Grandpa and his older brother Perry worked hard on the farm, but still they found time to hunt. They got a coonhound from a widow who lived in nearby Edgar Springs, Missouri, and slowly accumulated coon pelts that winter. They also found a buyer

1

nearby—an old-timer who trapped the river and had an old wooden johnboat.

He became a friend of the family eventually, and during spring and summer the 2 boys used his boat to fish from. It wasn't much of a boat—something like a feed trough, really, with straight sides. It didn't maneuver well, and it didn't hold a course. But it floated, and that was the most important thing.

As Grandpa began to save money from the sale of coon hides and groundhog hides, which sold at 5¢ apiece for leather boot laces, he began to think of making his own boat. But with 7 children in the family, other things were needed more than a boat. Besides, getting the boat-building materials from a local sawmill would cost nearly $5, a real investment in that day.

When the old trapper made a new boat, Fred and Perry Dablemont got the old one. It leaked badly, but was usable. That was when they began getting really interested in the river and the things it had to offer.

At a young age, they learned to trap, to gig redhorse suckers, and to set trotlines for giant catfish that could be sold in local settlements. They also learned to hunt the mallards and wood ducks along the river, discovering that oak boughs arranged across the front of the wooden boat made it possible to float silently into the range of the largest flocks.

Grandpa turned 15 in 1913, and by then he was an avid turkey hunter. He hunted gobblers by scattering the birds from their roosts just after dark and then waiting for them to return to that gathering place at dawn. Flocks of 60 to 70 turkeys were common in the Ozarks, and it wasn't a real task to get one. With his muzzle loader shotgun, Grandpa kept the family supplied with meat. His mother allowed him to kill another turkey only when the last one had been completely eaten.

In the fall of 1913, a St. Louis surveyor passed through the Ozarks and made it known he was an avid hunter and very much interested in taking a wild gobbler. By this time, Fred Dablemont was gaining something of a reputation. Everyone knew the boy from the Piney River who sold catfish and coon hides. And more than one farm wife in the vicinity of Edgar Springs had graced a Sunday table with wild turkey bought for 5¢ from the young hunter.

The surveyor was directed to the Dablemont farm where he met

Vic Dablemont, a Frenchman who said assuringly, in broken English, "Dat lettle boy, he halp you keel de turkee."

The surveyor returned a week later with a breech-loading shotgun, fancy hunting clothes, and new confidence.

For Grandpa, it was a simple assignment. That evening he scattered the flock from a ridge that overlooked the river. The next day before dawn he situated the hunter in a makeshift blind right where the turkeys would regroup.

The first half dozen turkeys to return, young jakes with short beards, walked right up to the hidden hunter. He emptied both barrels, managing to kill what he swore was the biggest gobbler he'd ever laid eyes on. He was so happy he gave Grandpa the breech-loading Stevens as payment. Then the surveyor returned to the city with the story of a young hunter so gifted he could kill turkeys without calling. They just came to him in groups. Of course he didn't know the turkeys were simply regrouping at the spot they had last seen their comrades.

The hunter returned with a friend. Fred Dablemont, perhaps the first 15-year-old hunting guide in the state, helped them each bag a young gobbler. He was paid handsomely, and other hunters came to enlist his services. Later in the fall, he put 2 hunters in the front of his old boat, piled a blind on the front of it, and paddled them down the river into several flocks of ducks.

Because of his success, more and more clients called on him. Though most of the money had to go to the family, Grandpa was able to save enough to buy materials for his own boat.

The first boat was quite an experiment. Fred and his brother, Perry, were blessed with efficient hands, though they were something short of efficient carpenters. They knew somehow that the straight sides, which made a boat like a feed trough, had to be improved. But they didn't know how to go about it. Over the next 2 years, they built several boats, coming up with new ideas for each. Finally, they had what they thought was a perfect boat for the Big Piney and Gasconade.

Even at that, Grandpa would effect many more changes in the boat in the years to come. He continued to use his boats for trapping, fishing, and hunting the river, and occasionally he guided for a few hunters and fishermen who came from the city on weekends.

World War I interrupted everything. At 17, Grandpa had been out of school for 5 years, having gone only as far as the sixth grade.

He knew very little about the outside world, and he communicated poorly with his parents. His mother was nearly full-blooded Cree Indian, and his father was an ill-tempered Frenchman. When Vic Dablemont learned about the war, his reaction was strong. He had been born and raised in France and had stowed away on a ship to Canada before he was 20.

When war broke out, he urged his son to go fight for France, "my countree'." That was the furthest thing from the youngster's mind, and he was beaten because he refused. Days later, Grandpa received his notice to report for the U.S. armed service. He knew little of such things, and assumed that it was the doing of his father.

He headed for the Big Piney with his dog, essential supplies, and a rolling-block Stevens .22 caliber rifle.

To throw off anyone who might follow, he headed upstream, toward the Big Piney headwaters, paddling against the current and pulling his johnboat over shoals he couldn't float.

For 8 months, Grandpa lived on the upper Piney, learning a great deal more about the outdoors than some men have the opportunity to learn in a lifetime. During the summer and fall, he lived on the river, sleeping in large caves with only his dog for company. Finally, he came to know a farmer named Harris and did part-time work for the man in the winter in return for a place to stay, an old room in the barn.

Finally, Fred Dablemont enlisted under an assumed name. Soon afterward he confessed everything. After 2 years of service, he received an honorable discharge and returned to the Big Piney with a good deal more knowledge of the world around him.

He went back to the Harris farm and part-time work. The first thing he did was build a new johnboat to carry out his plans. Fred Dablemont knew what he wanted to do. With his knowledge of the river, he figured he could make a good living by trapping, guiding hunters, and fishing commercially.

In 1919, he married Harris' daughter, Tollie, and the newlyweds built their first home, a 3-room cabin on the upper Piney. The home was furnished with beds, tables, and chairs that Grandpa made. Throughout his life, he believed in buying only what he could not make himself.

His work was always very efficient, though it sometimes lacked a little in appearance. To this day, I remember him rocking away in

4

an old rocking chair that he'd made, telling me stories by the light of a kerosene lantern about years long past.

Until his death in 1970, Grandpa lived exactly as he'd done in 1917. His homes were small, always on the river or creek, where he could keep a half-dozen johnboats at a time.

He never enjoyed the luxury of running water. They had the river nearby, a good well, and an outdoor john with a small heat stove—sort of luxurious for the Ozarks.

His home was heated by a wood-burning cook stove in the kitchen and a pot-bellied wood stove in the combination living

room-bedroom. He didn't need or want electricity. The house was lighted by a pair of kerosene lanterns. He believed in getting to bed early anyway, always turning in an hour or so after dark and rising every day an hour before sunrise.

He never used a power tool. He had a good draw knife, a couple of planes, several types of handsaws, a brace and bit, and an assortment of wood rasps.

Throughout his life he took great care of all his belongings, from minnow seines and steel traps to the tools he used building his boats. In the corners of his home hung well-oiled traps, a pair of hip boots, a rolled-up seine. Trotline spools and boat paddles sat beneath them. Usually 2 or 3 guns hung in handmade gun racks. All of them were loaded, always. Grandpa lived in an era when loaded guns were sometimes needed quickly, and he never forgot that. His children were raised knowing that every gun was loaded, and they never forgot it. Over the years, there was never a gun accident in the family.

The johnboat contributed indirectly to raising many a family in which trapping, fishing, and guiding were the major sources of income. Some rivermen earned income from johnboats directly by building and selling them.

Grandpa never thought he would be making his boats for sale. But before his death at the age of 73, my grandfather had built and sold just over 1,600 wooden johnboats and more than 3,000 sassafras paddles.

Chapter 2

Techniques of Building Johnboats

The johnboats Grandpa built in the 1920's and 1930's were crude. I was always amazed in later years at his ability to cut a seat to fit perfectly an unfinished boat by just looking at it.

Late in his life, Grandpa began to use measurements and precise angles. But most of his boats were built from memory and were improved through trial and error.

Most of the rivermen were like that. They were interested in efficiency and not too concerned with appearance. Those early johnboats must have looked fairly ragged.

It was hard to get good lumber. Boards often had a layer of bark on one edge. But of course the builder was happy to get scraps at low cost to build seats and live wells out of.

When a side board had a loose knot, Grandpa would remove it, tar it heavily, then replace it, and perhaps tack a leather patch over it to hold it securely in place.

The bottoms of those johnboats were made of pine boards. Usually the boards were 4 to 8 inches wide. They were nailed on crossways, with a crack left between each board and the next one. This crack was about ⅛ inch, the thickness of a pocket-knife blade. When the boat was soaked with water, the bottom boards would swell and seal tightly.

Some of the boat builders chose to tongue-and-groove those bottom boards and put some type of sealer between them. This idea emerged when power tools came on the scene, but it wasn't really much of an improvement. If the bottom boards were placed too closely together, the subsequent swelling would cause them to buck and crack. And the sealer was only good as long as the boat was soaked up. If the bottom ever dried out, it would shrink some. Then some of the sealer would come loose.

Of course in years back, boats seldom left the river. They were customarily chained to a tree along the river so they were readily accessible. Though they weren't likely to dry out, they were subject to decay. Algae growing on the boat worsened the situation.

My father, defying tradition, seldom left a boat in the river. Normally he would return boats to our home and keep bottoms sealed by placing burlap sacks, which he then kept wet, in the bottoms of the boats. In the summer, the boats were kept in the shade. Every few days, somebody had to check to be sure the sacks were good and wet.

A riverman from the 1920's and 1930's was happy to get 2 years' use out of a johnboat with the heavy use it was given. On larger streams, where rocks and shallow shoals weren't a problem, a boat lasted longer. My father aimed at getting 4 or 5 years out of his boats. To do that, he treated the bottoms with wood preservative and painted the boats each year. The boat we called Old Paint, a sentimental favorite of mine, lasted over 10 years.

Dad had one substantial advantage that Grandpa didn't have: Dad could get very good lumber. In 1920, Grandpa was happy to get any kind of material that was reasonably sound.

Early builders of johnboats were tempted to nail the bottom boards tightly together, rather than leave the required spaces between them. The result of nailing boards too close together was a bottom so tightly swollen that half the boards bucked up or down. It is absolutely necessary to leave the space between bottom boards. The boards swell tremendously, and the johnboat can be soaked up tightly in only a few hours.

Bottom boards must be of very good material. The edges must be straight and smooth and the boards well-seasoned.

The same is true of the boards used in the sides of a johnboat. They must be straight, seasoned, and unchecked. A crack in a side board can ruin a boat. My dad has always claimed that the sides are mostly responsible for leaks in later years.

Putting the tapered bow between the sides of the johnboat was a tricky job until Grandpa began using what he called "forming braces." He nailed the boat sides to these temporary braces as one of the first steps in building the johnboat. Then the ends were drawn together by tightening a rope around each end.

After Grandpa nailed on the bottom and nailed the end pieces and center braces in place, he removed the ropes and then the temporary forming braces, which would be used again and again. Grandpa came up with a set of forming braces for 12-foot boats and a set each for 15-, 16-, 17-, and 19-foot boats. Each set varied a little in size and angles.

Another important improvement in johnboats was the addition of keels, or "rudders" as my grandfather called them. The pair of 1-inch by 2-inch strips, running the length of the boat and nailed to the outside bottom about 15 inches apart, accomplished many things. These strips helped a boat run straight as it was paddled. They also gave added strength to the bottom and absorbed much of the abuse from rocky shoals.

But since there is an angle, or rake, in the bottom of the boat at each end, the rudders had to be bent. Grandpa accomplished this by sawing about halfway through the one-by-two's (on the side to be nailed against the bottom) at the spot where the bend was necessary. He made 3 cuts, each about ½ inch from the next, and placed the incised side against the boat bottom. He boiled a big container of water, placed burlap sacks on each rudder where a bend was to be made, and then poured on the steaming water a little at a time. In 10 to 15 minutes, the rudders could be bent at both ends without breaking, and nailed down.

In years past, rivermen put live wells in their boats. These were bottomless boxes, usually 1 foot by 2 foot, sealed tightly with tar, then sealed to the boat's floor, which became the live well's bottom. Two holes were drilled in the floor, inside the box. These could be kept plugged most of the time. But when the plugs were removed, the well held 5 to 6 inches of water, an adequate place to keep fish, or (if the holes were covered with screen) small minnows used for bait. It was a real job to keep bait alive in a bucket on a

LIVE WELL

LEATHER HINGES

CUTAWAY OF LIVE WELL

HOLES IN BOTTOM

hot summer day. But in a live well, with fresh water circulating in from the bottom, bait would stay alive for days. This was a tremendous aid for a commercial trotline fisherman, who seldom used dead bait.

A live well in the center of the boat had a lid, hinged with leather straps, and at times it served as a seat.

When the live well was not in use, the holes in the bottom of it could be plugged, and the well used as a storage compartment.

The early johnboats were fitted with board seats with one side-to-side brace. But my dad, when building his own boats in the 1950's, saw an opportunity to use space beneath seats as storage compartments. He made many of his boats with dry storage space beneath one or two seats.

It was early in the 1960's that Dad decided on using a plywood bottom for his johnboats, building a sealed craft that wouldn't have to be kept "soaked up."

The coming of butyl rubber in large containers provided Dad with a suitable agent for tightly sealing a craft. But he had doubts about the longevity of a plywood bottom.

Experimenting with exterior plywood, Dad found he could expect about 5 years of service from a ⅜-inch plywood bottom. He could get more years from a half-inch bottom, but the boat was heavier.

The best material was ⅜-inch marine plywood. Its great strength took the blows of a rocky shoal, yet kept the weight of a boat reasonably light. We always used the exterior plywood because marine plywood is very expensive. So Dad was building a boat that had 50 or 60 dollars worth of material in it and required 12 to 15 hours of work.

My grandfather, growing old by then, was building the last of his boats and couldn't see putting that kind of expense into them. He also thought a fellow was getting lazy when he had to have a permanently sealed boat that required no soaking to keep it tight. It was very little trouble, as he saw it, to keep one soaked up. And anyone who worried about the boat being too heavy was a bit of a weakling, he figured.

But when Dad decided he had considerably improved the johnboat by using a plywood bottom, almost everyone who bought boats from him preferred it.

A johnboat with a plywood bottom can last many years if you store it properly when it's not in use. You may get 10 or 15 years of service from a johnboat if you store it in a dry basement, garage, or shed. If you must keep the boat outside, turn it upside down and keep it covered with a tarpaulin. Dad says more damage is done to the boat by the heat of the sun than by rain, wind, and snow. If the wood is exposed each day to the heat of the sun, the wood dries and shrinks so badly that the seams can begin to leak.

Of course you should always store the boat on sawhorses or blocks off the ground and perfectly level to keep it from warping.

What wood makes the best johnboat? It's difficult to say. Our family has always used yellow pine because it is fairly light, strong, and resistant to cracking. Dad often used white pine for the bottom boards.

For ends, it's best to use good strong oak, though 2-inch-thick pine will work.

I'm not saying pine is the best material for a johnboat, but other lumber may be hard to get or too expensive. Some johnboat builders in years past used mahogany boards for the boat sides, but that material, though strong and not likely to crack, is far too expensive today.

At one time, lumber from the tupelo (black gum) was used for the bottom boards. This was fairly good material because it was hard and had little grain. But it's very difficult to put a nail through.

Cypress is said to be the best possible wood for boat building. It doesn't soak up much water and seems to resist rotting indefinitely. But cypress is also somewhat soft and is ground away by dragging over rocky shoals.

Redwood seems to resist water but has the drawback of being quite expensive.

If you use cypress, redwood, or mahogany, you will perhaps have a longer-lasting boat, but the expense will be far greater than that of pine.

Whatever wood is used, the life of a boat can be extended with wood preservative and annual paint jobs; this needs to be emphasized.

I firmly believe that screws in place of nails make a better, longer-lasting boat. My dad denies this, claiming his flooring nails or screw-nails are just as good, and much faster. Using screws in

11

the place of nails may add an additional day to the time required for completing the boat.

Nails that are off-line can ruin a boat, especially when you're nailing the bottom boards on. Be sure you don't get nails crooked and have them break out of the side boards. That kind of mistake opens the wood to water and decay. When you must remove a nail, plug the hole with a match-stick-size splinter of pine that's coated with glue, tar, or butyl rubber and driven into the hole with a hammer.

Many regions of the country developed wooden boats of distinctive styles. None was more heralded than the White River johnboats that made southwest Missouri popular with float fishermen.

The White and James Rivers had many boat builders and many float-fishing outfitters. One widely known organizer of White River float trips was a Branson resident named Jim Owens. He was a promoter who attracted fishermen to the Ozarks, and he developed a profitable business for guides and boat builders.

The action started sometime in the 1920's, and Jim Owens got involved in 1933. He worked out a system with the Missouri Pacific Railroad. Guides and fishermen embarked on the James River at Galena, Missouri, then floated into the White and down to Branson. It was a 5-day trip. When the float was over, Owens sent his boats back on the railroad via a special flatcar fitted with side poles, which could haul 16 boats.

Townsend Godsey, a writer who has lived in southwest Missouri many years and once taught journalism at School of the Ozarks College, did much research on those White River float trips. He talked to many of the old-timers who died when I was just a boy.

I talked to Godsey at length about the White River johnboat.

"Jim Owens was a promoter," he said, "but Charlie Barnes built the johnboats and worked for Jim as a guide."

In interviews with Charlie Barnes, Godsey learned that johnboats used at the turn of the century for gigging were only about 2 feet wide and nearly 30 feet long. They were pushed by giggers using long gigs, and they were known as "redhorse runners" after the big fish sought by giggers. Gigs in that day were not the fine-pronged gigs of today. They were made from heavy metal, and the tines (or prongs) were nearly as big around as a pencil. A gig of this sort could be used to push a boat, without dulling the tines much.

12

Godsey said native giggers sometimes crowded bass against a rock bank, or banged against rocky shoals with gig poles and caused the fish to frantically try to jump over the boat. Side boards along the far side of the boat caused bass to fall into the boat. According to Barnes, there was a time when fish were so thick that giggers could get several dozen bass a night in such a manner. The method is now illegal.

For gigging, Barnes built 20-foot johnboats, about 3 feet wide at the center. He built shorter boats for float fishing. His boats were much different from my grandfather's johnboats. Charlie used 3 20-foot boards, 12 inches wide, for a boat bottom. They ran lengthwise, and were tongue-and-grooved and sealed and joined. There's uncertainty about what material was used to seal the boat, but one man who worked with Barnes said he remembers using thin rags between the tongue-and-groove joints. Wooden strips—½ by 2½ inches—ran the full length of the boat to cover the floorboard joints from the outside (bottom). These served as rudders or keels.

The White River boats were reinforced on the inside by wrought-iron ribs made from old wagon tires. These ribs held the shape of the sides without any center seats, and gave the boat considerable strength.

Charlie Barnes built about 300 boats, the last of them in the mid 1950's. One of his old boats, or what is left of it, is on display at the School of the Ozarks College near Branson, Missouri.

Jim Owens, who drew "furriners" to the Ozarks to float the beautiful White, fought hard against the coming of dams that destroyed the spectacular stream.

Later, Owens went into the real-estate business and became wealthy.

The smallmouth that once teemed in the White are gone, and the cold water that flows from Tablerock Lake is now periodically stocked with trout. The trout lake, called Taneycomo, is jammed with fishermen most of the time, and outboard motors roar up and down it. Taneycomo flows past Branson, between Tablerock and the next lake downstream, Bull Shoals. It is overdeveloped, with homes and cottages crowding the shores, and poor septic systems beginning to add pollution. Low oxygen during the summer is also beginning to cause trout die-offs, and friction.

The area is billed as an Ozark playground. But it grows crowded and uglier as developers and entrepreneurs take advantage of the tourist trade.

Where the White, now buried, once flowed quiet and serene, abounding in beauty, there are now rows of trailer homes, drab surroundings, and too many people for the recreational resource to support. Some people say that all the Ozarks will someday be thus. But the progress and wealth that come from reservoirs and dams have transformed the White River area into something some Ozark natives did not want to see.

Chapter 3

How to Build Your Own Authentic 14-Foot Wooden Johnboat

My dad, Farrel Dablemont, may be the last builder of wooden johnboats in the Ozarks. He learned to build the boats by helping and watching my grandfather in the 1930's. Dad and his brothers and father lived on the Big Piney River, where they rented boats and guided floatfishermen from the 1930's well into the 1960's.

Dad has estimated he built nearly 200 johnboats on his own since 1948. In the early 1950's, he built and delivered johnboats to floatfishing resorts on the Gasconade, Big Piney, and Bourbeuse Rivers in Missouri and sold his boats to commercial fishermen on the Osage and Missouri Rivers. Now in his early 50's, he continues to build 5 or 6 johnboats each year.

Besides building the johnboats, Dad is an expert in handling them. He has the same dexterity that the old-time river guides were famous for.

On the following pages, he demonstrates in step-by-step photographs (accompanied by accurate plans) how to build an authentic wooden johnboat. The process is complete whether your aim is to build the version with the plywood bottom (which can be stored dry) or the older version with a slat bottom (which must be kept wet).

A Most Important Preliminary

The key ingredient in producing a well-formed johnboat is the temporary forming brace. You'll need 2. You can use scrap lumber to build them (as was done with those in the photo), but their dimensions must be accurate. The forming braces will be removed late in the building process.

15

Dad prefers a 15-degree angle in the sides of the forming braces. For each forming brace, cut 2 1″ x 10″ boards at a 15-degree angle as shown, and nail them together solidly with 2 or more 1″ x 4″ or 1″ x 6″ cross strips. These forming braces must be very strong.

For this 14-foot boat, the bottom of the front brace should measure 32 inches across; the back brace should measure 34 inches across. (See Drawings 1A and 1B, and Photo 1.)

Photo 1

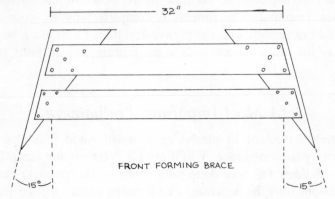

Drawing 1A

16

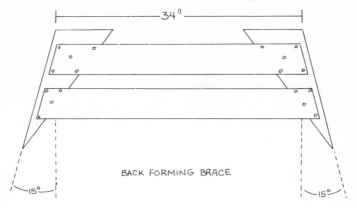

BACK FORMING BRACE

Drawing 1B

Building Your Johnboat, Step by Step

First Stage: Set up 2 sturdy 5-foot-wide sawhorses, 8 feet apart, and level each one perfectly, as in Photo 2. During the boat build-

Photo 2

ing, the sawhorses must remain level.

Important note: The boat is built mostly upside down on the sawhorses.

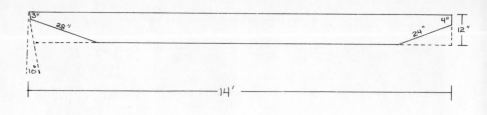

Drawing 2

Photo 3

Second Stage: Measure and cut side boards as in Drawing 2. The front of the board, which will be the bow, should be angled 10 degrees from the vertical. If you are using a 12-inch-wide board, the front of the board will be cut off at 3 inches from the top and the back will be cut off at 4 inches. But if you are using 14-inch boards (thereby eliminating the need to add a top strip later), the front will be cut off at 5 inches and the back at 6 inches. (See Drawing 2 and Photos 3, 4, 5, and 6.) Now you have produced 2 completed side boards. (See Photo 7.)

Photo 4

Photo 5   *Photo 6*

Photo 7

Third Stage: Nail 1″ x 2″ strips to the lower inside edge of each side board. Drawing 3 shows the pattern for the right side board.

PROPER ATTACHMENT OF 1×2 STRIPS TO SIDES

Drawing 3

The left side board is a mirror image. The edge of the strip must extend beyond the side board's edge by about ⅛ inch as shown in Drawing 4 and Photo 8. This arrangement is essential for later

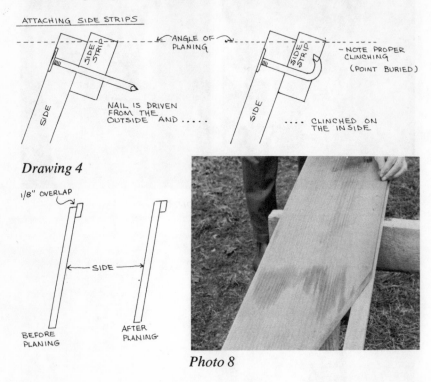

ATTACHING SIDE STRIPS

SIDE STRIP

ANGLE OF PLANING

NOTE PROPER CLINCHING
(POINT BURIED)

SIDE

NAIL IS DRIVEN FROM THE OUTSIDE AND .....

SIDE

.... CLINCHED ON THE INSIDE

Drawing 4

1/8" OVERLAP

←— SIDE —→

BEFORE PLANING

AFTER PLANING

Photo 8

producing a flat surface (by planing) to meet the boat's bottom. Use No. 6 resin-treated box nails, one every 4 inches and staggered on the 1″ x 2″ side strips. Clinch (bend over) the nails on the inside, and countersink the points with a dull punch. (See Drawing 4 and Photos 9 and 10.) Side boards with strips nailed to lower edge are shown in Photo 11. Note that strips end short of side-board ends, to make room for later insertion of boat's end pieces.

Photo 9

Photo 10

Photo 11

Fourth Stage: Attach the side boards to the forming braces. One brace is placed 48 inches from the front of the side boards, and the other is placed 44 inches from the back of the side boards. (See Photos 12, 13, and 14). The forming braces should butt against

Photo 12

Photo 13

Photo 14

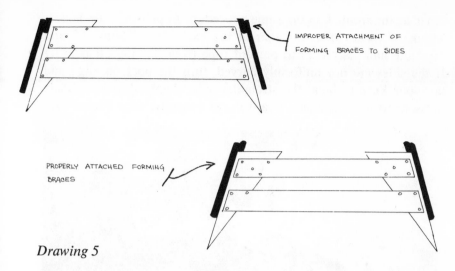

IMPROPER ATTACHMENT OF FORMING BRACES TO SIDES

PROPERLY ATTACHED FORMING BRACES

Drawing 5

the 1″ x 2″ strips, so the side boards touch the forming braces. (See Drawing 5.) Fasten the side boards solidly to the forming braces with 2-inch screws, 4 screws for each brace. (The screws and forming braces can be easily removed later, when it is time to put in permanent braces.)

Fifth Stage: Now with the boat bottom up, use a rope and an adjustable knot to pull the side boards to within 23 inches of each

Photo 15

Photo 16

23

other at the front. Use the same procedure to pull the side boards within 25 inches of each other at the back. (See Photos 15 and 16. Note nail placement to prevent rope from slipping off board.) If the sides are not uniformly curved, turn the boat on edge and use your knee to bend the straighter side. Apply slow but steady pressure to make the side board curve properly. (See Photo 17.)

Photo 17

This problem seldom arises if the boards are matched and straight.

24

Sixth Stage: Now you're ready to cut and fit the end pieces. These should be 2 inches thick. Fitting them can be difficult because the edges must be not only properly angled from top to bottom but also beveled slightly from front to back to fit snugly between the side boards. (See Drawing 6.) Precise

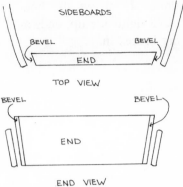

Drawing 6

measuring is the key. (See Photos 18 and 19.) Nail each end piece

Photo 18

Photo 19

between the side boards with No. 8 screw nails, and use 5 or 6 nails in each side. The ends are point of much stress and the joints must hold tightly. (See Photo 20.)

Photo 20

Photo 21 shows the boat at this stage right-side up, ends and forming braces in.

Photo 21

Seventh Stage: Prepare the lower edges of the side boards to receive the boat's bottom. The curve of the boat makes the lower edges of the side boards angle inward. With a good plane, you can readily make both sides perfectly flat. (See Photo 22 and Drawing

Photo 22

4.) To check the accuracy of your planning, run a flat board along

Photo 23

26

the bottom. (See Photo 23.) Dips or humps will show up, and more planing can make the lower edges of the side boards very flat. Also plane the bottom edge of both end pieces so the bottom will fit snugly there. (See Photo 24.)

Photo 24

Eighth Stage: The rake (slope) of the boat in front and back creates an abrupt angle in the lower edge of the side boards. Before the bottom can be fastened in place, you must reduce the abruptness of the angles on both side boards, front and back, by planing off an 8-inch curve, about ½ inch deep. (See Photo 25.) (See Drawing 7.)

Photo 25

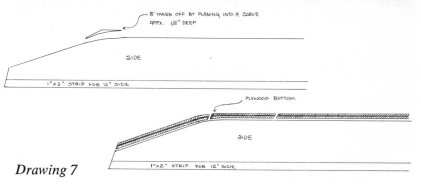

8" TAKEN OFF BY PLANING INTO A CURVE
APPX. 1/2" DEEP

SIDE

1"X2" STRIP FOR 12" SIDE

PLYWOOD BOTTOM

SIDE

Drawing 7

1"X2" STRIP FOR 12" SIDE

MODERN METHOD USING PLYWOOD BOTTOM

27

Ninth Stage: If you have a 10-foot section of plywood, you need to make only 2 splices, or joints, in the bottom. If you have standard 8-foot plywood, you'll need to make 3 joints. (See Drawing 8, especially bevel details.) The bottom pieces must be beveled

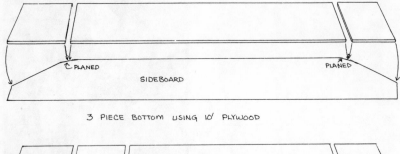

3 PIECE BOTTOM USING 10' PLYWOOD

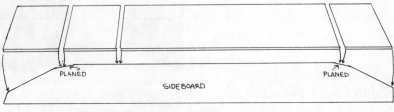

4 PIECE BOTTOM USING 8' PLYWOOD

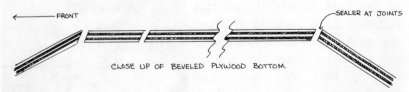

CLOSE UP OF BEVELED PLYWOOD BOTTOM

Drawing 8

and carefully fitted together. The slope of each bevel should point toward the back of the boat, to keep any small lip from catching on a rock or snag. The bevel is made by setting the power saw's blade at an angle. This angle may be varied slightly, but should be close to 45 degrees. (See Photo 26.)

Photo 26

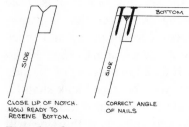

CLOSE UP OF NOTCH. NOW READY TO RECEIVE BOTTOM.

CORRECT ANGLE OF NAILS

Drawing 9

Tenth Stage: When the plywood sections have been properly shaped to form the bottom of the boat but *not* fastened in place, put them aside temporarily and cut a notch the full length of each side between the side board and side-board strip, to form a small channel for the sealer compound. (See Drawing 9 and Photo 27 and 28.) Dad cuts the notch with a hammer and an old hunting knife, but you might prefer a chisel in place of the knife.

Photo 28

Photo 27

29

Photo 29

Photo 30

Eleventh Stage: Now you're ready to permanently fasten the bottom, section by section. Using the butyl rubber silicone sealer, fill each notch liberally and spread the sealer with a putty knife. (See Photos 29 and 30.) Now comes the most difficult and most important part of building your johnboat. The bottom sections must be nailed exactly in place, largest section first. The nails must angle precisely into the slanting side boards. (See Drawing 9.) Use No. 6 screw-nails (or flooring nails) and space them 2 inches apart. (See Photo 31.) If a nail breaks out of the side board, your boat will leak slightly; the side board is also more apt to crack and split, and the side will decay quicker.

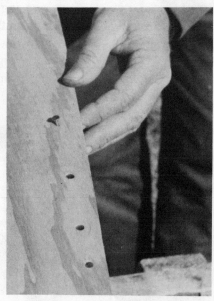

Photo 31

30

Twelfth Stage: When you finish nailing the main bottom section of plywood to the side boards, nail the same section to the adjacent side-board strips. Use No. 6 screwnails (flooring nails), place them 2 inches apart, and stagger them from the other row of nails. (See Photo 32 and Drawing 10.) As

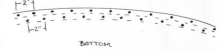

BOTTOM

NAILING BOTTOM TO SIDES. STAGGER NAILS.
Drawing 10

you apply the other sections of the plywood bottom, liberally apply the sealer to the face of all joints and also seal the ends well. (Photos 33, 34, and 35.)

Photo 32

Photo 33

Photo 34

Photo 35

Thirteenth Stage: The bottom is now in place, but it's not firm and solid yet. The keels, or rudders, come next, and they are a part of making the bottom stable. (See Photo 36.) Be sure they will be

Photo 36   Photo 37

long enough to reach both ends after bending. At the points where the keels must bend, make 3 saw cuts ⅓ of the way through. (See Photo 37.) Then turn the cuts toward the boat bottom. (See Drawing 11.) Arrange these keels about 10 or 12 inches apart, and be

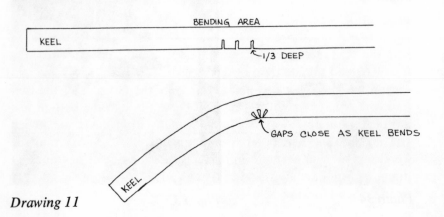

Drawing 11

sure they are lined up perfectly straight. (See Photo 38.) They

Photo 38

help the boat maintain its course. If one or both are crooked, the boat will tend to fade right or left as it floats.

Nail the keels in place first across only the flat part of the bottom with No. 4 box nails. They will come through the bottom just a little, so you'll need to clinch them tightly from the inside. When you do this, the nail point is countersunk (bent down) into the wood with a hammer and dull punch so it never catches on anything. Proper clinching also makes the keel-to-bottom bond very strong. (See Drawing 12.)

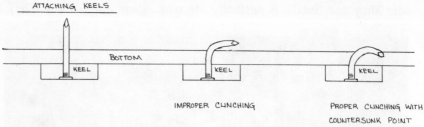

BOTTOM

KEEL   KEEL   KEEL

IMPROPER CLINCHING

PROPER CLINCHING WITH
COUNTERSUNK POINT

Drawing 12

Fourteenth Stage: Before you can nail the rest of each keel in place, you must bend each to fit the rake of the boat bottom. The shallow saw cuts made at the 2 bending points of each keel help you to do this. But you must also wrap each keel in burlap or other heavy fabric at the bending points and pour on boiling water for 10 or 15 minutes to make the keel strips pliable. (See Photo 39.) Then remove the burlap, slowly bend the keels down, and nail them in place. Use No. 4 box nails to secure keels, 1 nail every 4 inches, staggered. Of course the keels at each end are nailed into the end pieces of the boat, bow and stern. When the nailing is finished, the keel adds strength to the bottom of the boat. Clinch nails as shown in Drawing 12. With keels completely nailed in place, boat looks as it does in Photo 40.

Photo 40

34

Photo 41

If you should break or crack a keel while bending it, use a strip of pliable metal to cover 10 or 12 inches of the keel across the bending point. Use screws to hold the metal in place. (See Photo 41.) If you will use the boat in shallow rocky water where the bottom of the boat is constantly grinding against the substrate, it's a good idea to add such a reinforcing metal strip at all 4 bending points anyway.

Fifteenth Stage: When the keels are in place and the boat is still bottom up, use a saw, a plane, and some wood files to trim the edges of the bottom to a perfect fit, exactly flush with the side boards.

Photo 42

Sixteenth Stage: Now turn the boat topside up, with the bottom resting on the sawhorses. (See Photo 42 and note that forming braces are still in place.) If you have used 14-inch side boards, your boat is deep enough for most streams. But if you have used 12-inch side boards, you must add a 2-inch strip at the top of both sides. Don't try to nail these on in

an ordinary way. Nail 1 end of the 2-inch strip to the end piece at the bow. Then drill holes down through the strip and into the top of the side board. (See Photo 43.) The forming braces, which are still in place, help you to make the strip fit exactly along the side board.

Photo 43

Drill a hole about every 4 to 6 inches, and drive a 3-inch finishing nail (No. 10) into each as you go. (See Photo 44 and Drawing 13.)

Photo 44

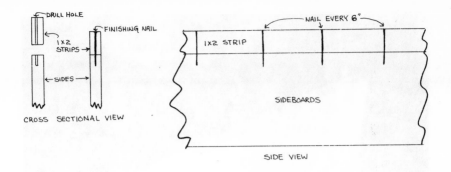

DRILL HOLE

FINISHING NAIL

1x2 STRIPS

SIDES

CROSS SECTIONAL VIEW

NAIL EVERY 6"

1x2 STRIP

SIDEBOARDS

SIDE VIEW

Drawing 13

Seventeenth Stage: When the strips have been added to the top of the side boards (see Photo 45), trim the side boards at bow and

Photo 45

stern so they are flush with the end pieces. If you want to use a small motor on your boat, you may want to reinforce the stern's end board with a pine board or a piece of plywood. (See Photos 46 and 47.)

37

Photo 46

Photo 47

38

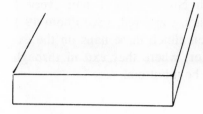

BEFORE PLANING

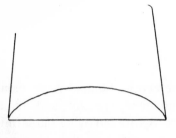

AFTER PLANING

Eighteenth Stage: Your johnboat has 3 joints between bottom sections if you used 8-foot plywood. Cut a pine strip (½″ x 2″ or ½″ x 3″) to fit across each joint *inside* the boat. Plane down the sharp edges of the upper side. (See Drawing 14.) The rounded strips are not apt to cause you to trip. Each strip runs the entire length of its joint (the width of the

Drawing 14

Photo 48

boat). Apply sealer liberally to the joint before installing each strip. (See Photo 48.) Fasten each strip

Photo 49

with No. 4 nails, 1 nail every 4 inches, staggered. (See Photo 49.) Then clinch those nails on the exterior, where they extend through the boat bottom.

Nineteenth Stage: Now you're about ready to cut and fit the seats. Before removing the forming braces, nail in the permanent braces on which the seats will rest. If there is to be no dry compartment under a seat, use a 1" x 4" permanent cross brace under the center of the seat. (See Photo 50.)

Photo 50

If there is to be a dry compartment under the seat, use two braces (1" x 8" or 1" x 10") and a Masonite or plywood bottom. (See Drawing 15 and Photos 51 and 52.) The seats are centered on these permanent braces, and there can be some slight variation here.

The second seat from the back should be centered about 6 inches

Photo 51

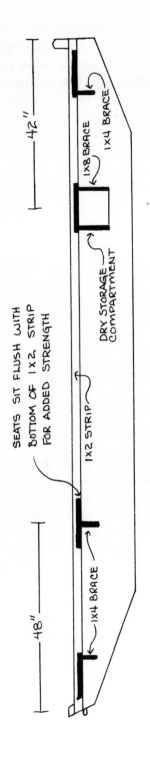

SEATS SIT FLUSH WITH
BOTTOM OF 1x2 STRIP
FOR ADDED STRENGTH

1x8 BRACE

1x4 BRACE

DRY STORAGE
COMPARTMENT

1x2 STRIP

1x4 BRACE

42"

48"

SEAT PLACEMENT FOR 14' BOAT

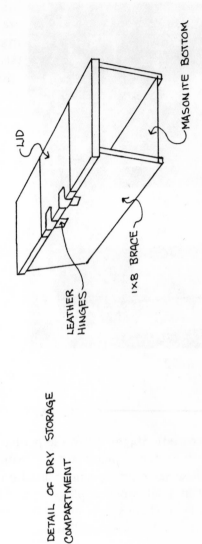

DETAIL OF DRY STORAGE
COMPARTMENT

LID

LEATHER
HINGES

1x8 BRACE

MASONITE BOTTOM

Drawing 15

behind the rear temporary forming brace. The second seat from the front should be 6 inches ahead of the front temporary forming brace.

Be sure the permanent braces are nailed in so that the top of each brace aligns with the seam between the 12-inch side board and the 1" x 2" top strip. Use No. 8 resin-treated nails for seats and braces.

Photo 52

Twentieth Stage: When the permanent braces are solidly installed for the proper placement of seats, remove the forming braces. (These same braces can be used on a future boat or boats.)

Cut small wooden plugs to seal the screw holes in the side of the boat where you removed the forming braces. The butyl rubber sealer applied to a small wooden plug will seal these holes tightly.

Twenty-first Stage: Cut and fit seats (1" x 10" or 1" x 12" boards) to lie on top of the center braces. Nail the 2 center seats in. (See Drawing 15). When this is done, the seat will be about 1 inch under the top of the side strip. The bottom of the seat will be flush with the seam between the 12-inch side board and the added 1" x 2" strip.

That 1-inch "lip" of wood above the seat keeps rods, reels, and other gear from slipping off the seat into the river.

Twenty-second Stage: Now you cut and fit the end seats. They should also align at their bottom edge with the seam where the 2-inch strip joins the 12-inch side board. End seats should be 14 to 18 inches wide, each nailed into the end of the boat and supported by a 1″ x 4″ brace. Be sure you put the desired eye bolt into the front end (see Photo 53) before nailing in the end seats. (See Photo 54.)

Photo 53

Photo 54

43

Photo 55

Twenty-third Stage: Trim and smooth end pieces (see Photo 55), and lightly plane off the sharp edges of the seats and sides to round them and prevent splintering.

Photo 56

Twenty-fourth Stage: The boat is now ready to paint. A good marine paint is highly resistant to water. If you don't want to use the higher-cost marine paint, use farm-implement paint or porch-and-deck paint. The best color is a drab green or dead grass (see Photo 56), and you can camouflage it if you like with a few sprays of brown and black paint from spray cans.

With any paint, mix ¾ pints of linseed oil with ¼ pint of paint for the primer coat. For the second coat (after the primer has dried), use the paint without adding linseed oil.

44

For Alternate Version With Slat Bottom

If you want to build the old-style river johnboat that must be kept "soaked up," follow the procedure just described right through the seventh stage. Then continue as follows:

Starting at the center, cut and nail on crossways ½″ x 6″ or ½″ x 8″ boards. (See Photo 57.) Use No. 6 resin-treated nails,

Photo 57

and drive 1 into the side board every 2 inches. Then drive another row of nails into the adjacent side-board strip, the same distance apart but staggered, *not* side by side with the nails in the other row.

Continue to add boards to the bottom, leaving space of 1/16″ to ⅛″ between boards. (See Photo 58.) If you are using 8-inch

Photo 58

boards, make those spaces a little wider than if you were using 6-inch boards. The swelling of an 8-inch board is greater.

When you get to the rake angle, front and rear, plane off the corner along a straight line, as shown in Photo 59 and Drawing 16. Then 1 board sits on the 8-inch planed area. This cross board

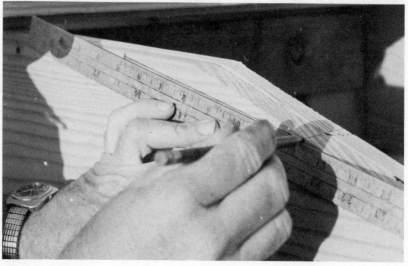

Photo 59

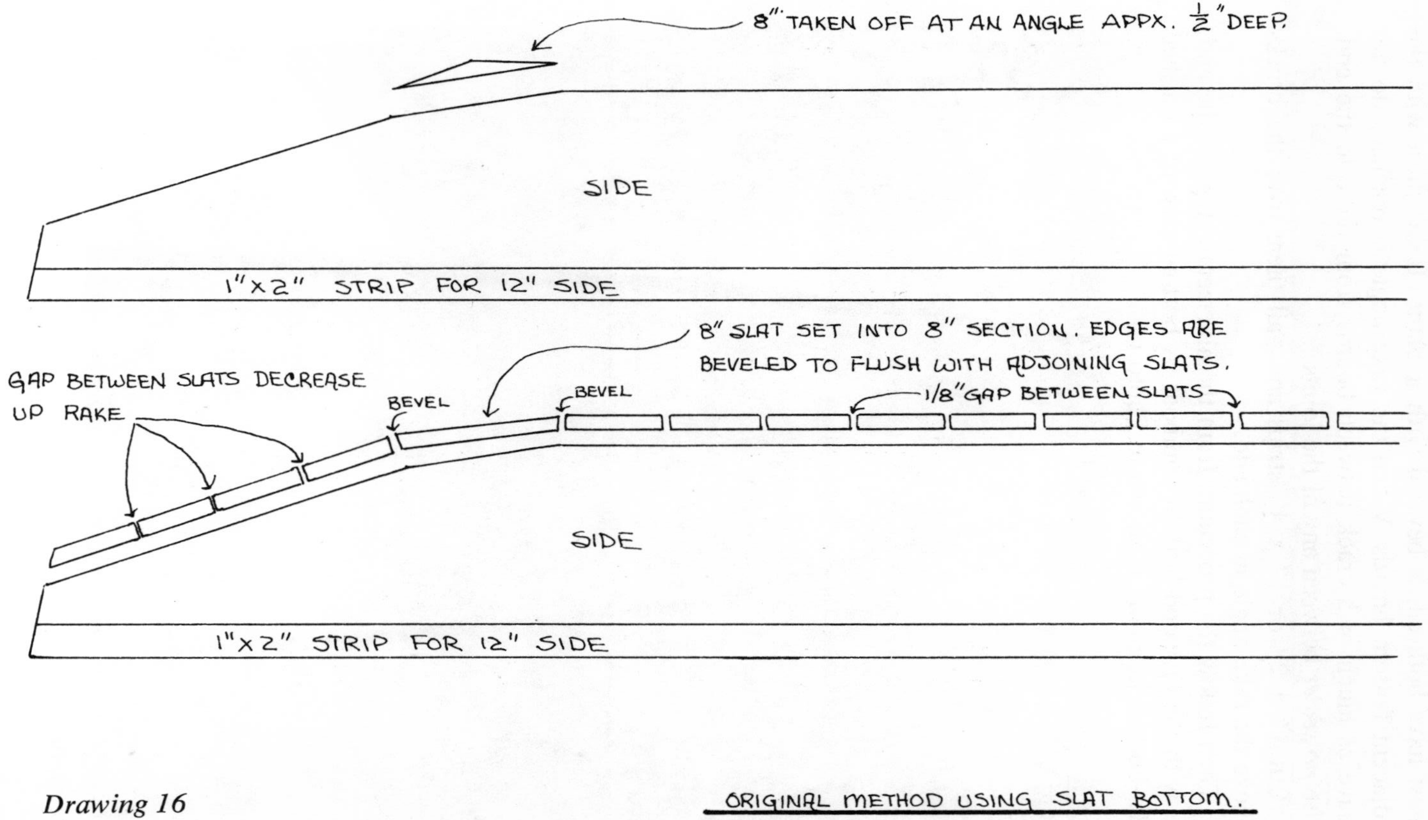

8" TAKEN OFF AT AN ANGLE APPX. $\frac{1}{2}$" DEEP.

SIDE

1" × 2" STRIP FOR 12" SIDE

8" SLAT SET INTO 8" SECTION. EDGES ARE
BEVELED TO FLUSH WITH ADJOINING SLATS.

1/8" GAP BETWEEN SLATS

BEVEL

SIDE

BEVEL

GAP BETWEEN SLATS DECREASE
UP RAKE

1" × 2" STRIP FOR 12" SIDE

ORIGINAL METHOD USING SLAT BOTTOM.

Drawing 16

must have both edges beveled with a plane. It fits flush with the adjacent bottom boards. When the rake angle is reached, do not leave as much of a crack between boards from there to the end. Use *no sealer* between any of the joints.

Cut 1″ x 2″ or 1″ x 4″ strips and nail them over the cracks above the rake angle in each end.

Then follow the procedure from the nineteenth stage to the end, as with the plywood-bottom johnboat. A bottom view of a finished slat-bottom johnboat is shown in Photo 60.

Photo 60

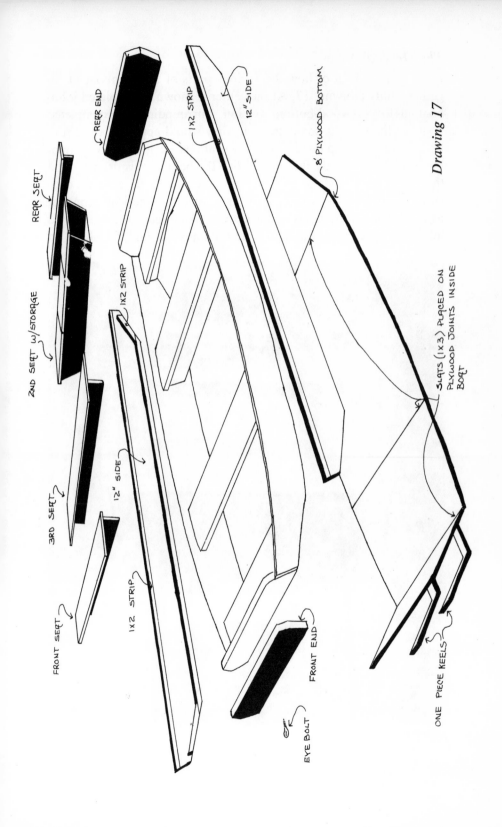

REAR END

REAR SEAT

1×2 STRIP

12" SIDE

8' PLYWOOD BOTTOM

2ND SEAT W/STORAGE

1×2 STRIP

SLATS (1×3) PLACED ON PLYWOOD JOINTS INSIDE BOAT

3RD SEAT

12" SIDE

FRONT SEAT

1×2 STRIP

FRONT END

EYE BOLT

ONE PIECE KEELS

Drawing 17

The Over-All View

For a general idea of how the various parts of the johnboat fit together, study Drawing 17. At the center is shown a completed johnboat in the plywood-bottom version. Surrounding the completed boat are the various components as they would appear if the entire boat suddenly "exploded." Slight variations occur. No two johnboats are ever exactly the same. With the help of this drawing and the foregoing drawings and photos, you should be able to construct a workmanlike example of the authentic American johnboat as it evolved on the rivers of the Ozarks. A closeup of a completed johnboat appears in Photo 61, and Photos 62 and 63 show an

Photo 61

Photo 62

overhead and a side view of johnboats under way. The jacket of
this book shows a fully loaded johnboat on an Ozark river.

Photo 63

Chapter 4

How Johnboats Compare With Other River Craft

It's not easy to compare the various craft that are used across the country today for floating, hunting, and fishing.

One difficulty is the tremendous diversity of streams, marshes, and lakes. Certain waters are not suitable for johnboats or canoes. Many rivers of the West fit into this category. And you must use your own judgment on large lakes. A calm body of water is never much of a problem. But during high winds, that same body of water becomes impossible. Northern rivers often require a good deal of portaging. Johnboats and larger canoes are impractical for such use.

Large rivers in the Midwest such as the Missouri, Ohio, Arkansas, and Mississippi are not for small craft. Expert canoeists often float them, but these large streams will fool the inexperienced floater with whirlpools, undercurrents, and unnoticed obstacles.

Dozens of drownings happen each year when people try to use small boats and canoes on major waterways and large lakes.

My grandfather used to tell me he could float the Big Piney River at flood stage, if he had to do it. But he was quick to add that he wasn't fool enough to do it unless he had to. Most of today's floaters underestimate the relentless and unstoppable power of even a small stream.

Floaters who enjoy the thrill of bouncing over a white-water shoal envision similar thrills in riding the current of a flooded river. But no one should float a flooded stream unless he absolutely must. Only experienced, capable floaters should even tackle rain-swollen waters. And larger, major rivers are not for recreational floating.

Large lakes are hazardous to small craft because of wave action and the wakes thrown by larger motor-powered boats.

When Norfolk Lake was constructed in the Missouri-Arkansas border in the 1940's wooden johnboats were built for use in the rough water of the large lake. They were powered then by small outboards. The boat builders found that the same boats used so well on rivers could be modified and used equally well on lakes.

My grandfather used the same basic design, but for lake johnboats he lengthened the craft, gave them greater width, and increased the height of the sides to 18 inches.

Grandpa was an avid trotliner. He made numerous trips each year to Norfolk, either trotlining by himself or guiding large parties. Thus, in the 1940's he put together some 18- and 20-foot johnboats. On small streams, he stayed with 14- to 16-foot lengths. For larger rivers like the White, the Gasconade, and the Osage, Grandpa built some slender 17- and 18-foot boats. For small farm ponds and creeks, he built several 12-foot boats; however, they were not very stable. He used the same basic design for boats of any length by varying angles and dimensions.

Johnboats are not suited for large motors. As a rule, any motor too large for a canoe is too large for a johnboat. Extra-large boats made for lakes are suitable for motors of 9 or 10 horsepower. But 14- to 16-foot boats should be powered by motors from 1.5 horsepower to 5 or 6 horsepower.

On small streams, such as the Buffalo in Arkansas, motors are neither necessary nor desirable. I can't imagine anyone taking a float on a scenic free-flowing stream and wanting a motor along. The peacefulness and quiet beauty of a stream are destroyed by the drone of a motor. A wild stream isn't a place for man's machinery. The river is slow at times, but it has much to offer those who will travel slowly and quietly.

Larger streams, especially those with little current, may be more appropriate for a motor, especially when upstream travel is necessary. Motors are more appropriate for small lakes.

Though I have seldom used outboards on our johnboats, I have often used the small battery-powered trolling motors, especially when I float to photograph wildlife. A trolling motor isn't much faster than a boat paddle, but it moves you along quietly and leaves your hands free to operate a camera.

When it's absolutely necessary to travel several miles in a hurry, it's good to know that a well-built johnboat can be powered by outboards. But I feel, as do many others, that most wild and scenic free-flowing streams should be off limits to motor-powered boats. It is a shame for the peace and solitude of nature's best work to be ruined by the drone of motors in the hands of someone too lazy to use a paddle.

In comparing the various small craft available for floating streams and small marshes and lakes, it is very difficult to make absolute statements about the advantages and disadvantages of each.

I can only give my own opinions, based on my own experiences. Other outdoor people with different experiences may arrive at different conclusions.

In the limited amount of guiding I did in my teens and years since, I've had an opportunity to float in everything from wooden and aluminum johnboats to canoes of aluminum and fiberglass to the later models of plastic. There were years when I floated more than a thousand miles. Now I probably average 400 or 500 river miles a year.

During the winter, when I'm hunting or photographing wildlife, I like to average 15 or 20 miles per day. During the summer, when I'm fishing or just enjoying the river, I average 10 to 15 miles a day.

Of course every river is different. On some small streams, 5 to 6 miles will take most of the day. When a stream is full, without a lot of obstacles and a good current, you may float 5 or 6 miles in a couple of hours.

I learned the most about canoes and the people who use them while I was working as a canoeing instructor at a summer camp in southern Missouri, and at the Buffalo National River. During several summers, I tried to teach canoeing to park visitors.

I could never understand why most canoeists seem to figure that the more miles you travel each day, the better. I think the key to enjoying a float trip is a leisurely pace, stopping from time to time on a gravel bar or exploring a cave in a nearby bluff.

By traveling quietly and even slowly, the river traveler gets to see the stream and many of the wildlife species that live along it. But

BOB MARTIN

if you make a mad dash for a take-out point with paddles banging against aluminum, you drive wild things—fish included—into secluded hiding places.

The johnboat was built years ago for a river traveler not too concerned with speed. He was a man with work to do. The ability of those early guides and trappers and commercial fishermen was a thing of wonder. Toughened, hard-working men, they could run a johnboat upstream over a shoal so strong you couldn't stand up in it. They could put the miles behind them when it was necessary, or paddle slowly with one hand.

If he knew what he was doing, he never switched sides with a paddle. Rivermen paddled all day from one side, and they could maneuver a boat for any distance without a splash or other sound. Many of them would slip along for long periods and never take the blade out of the water.

Outdoorsmen of that generation thought little about the weight of a johnboat. Most boats never left the river. Generally they were chained and locked to a tree where they were last used and where they would be needed again. Usually they weren't carried any distance overland.

That weight is the wooden johnboat's great disadvantage, especially now that floaters load and unload boats at a variety of access points. But the advantages of the wooden johnboat are many. It has tremendous stability, and it will hold a greater load than any other craft of comparable length. You can walk down the side of a johnboat like a tightrope, and fall out of it without capsizing.

The wooden johnboat is a quiet craft for river travel. If you drop something, the sound is minimal. If you're hunting or taking pictures, the wooden johnboat will make little noise as it slides over an object. If you hit a rock, you slide over it. Aluminum tends to hold as it grates against solid rock, and if it does slide, the noise can be heard a half mile away.

I would not try to evaluate each type of boat without using each for considerable amounts of time.

One of my favorite craft is a 19-foot Grumman square-stern canoe. I use it in the spring on many Ozark rivers because it floats high and is stable and easy to handle. It is noisy on shallow shoals, but then it is light and easy to carry when I want to reach rivers with poor access.

56

On windy days, I sacrifice that portability and turn to the 15-foot wooden johnboat. In a wind, the long light canoe is hard for me to control. The short and heavy johnboat holds a course much better in a strong wind.

The 15-foot johnboat is easy to camouflage by attaching a blind to the bow. A longer craft is harder to hunt or photograph from. But the greatest advantage of a wooden boat for some sportsmen might be its low price. It can be built for about $50 and two days of work. As I write this, a 17-foot johnboat made of aluminum is priced from $400 to $450. The 19-foot Grumman square-stern sells for about $550. And most 17-foot canoes sell for $350 or $400. I expect all those prices to increase.

The 19-foot square-stern is hard to get, but I'm convinced that in most respects it is far superior to small canoes. The 17-foot canoe has few advantages. It is light and fast, but it is also relatively unstable and will go over easily. It doesn't float any higher than the

19-footer, and it is used primarily by those who want to float fast and light, or those who float northern streams where portaging is necessary.

The double-ended 17-foot canoe is a craft I use only when I don't mind the possibility of getting wet. I never fill it with expensive equipment. This craft is unforgiving: make a mistake in it and you're wet. Lose your balance, turn sideways in a rough shoal, or start horseplaying, and you will go over in a hurry. I've seen beginning canoeists on average streams turn over half a dozen times on one trip. But an experienced canoeist may load the canoe fairly heavy and take a 2-day trip without incident. No matter how good you are, however, the 17-foot canoe can throw you. Expect it, and let that be your guide in determining what (and how much) you put in it.

Almost anyone who's done much floating in the 17-foot canoe can tell you about the times they've gone over. Where portaging is necessary, however, as in the north, the 17-foot canoe enjoys clear superiority to all others because of its light weight.

Square-stern canoes have an advantage over the double-enders, in that they are easier to turn. A double-end canoe has 18 inches of aluminum behind the paddler that creates resistance in turning. When the stern paddler is closer to the absolute rear point of the craft, as in the square-stern models, it is much easier to turn quickly. In a johnboat or square-stern canoe, I can backpaddle right up to an object on the bank. But in any double-end canoe, the space behind me prevents this maneuver. A 17-foot square-stern, which has 3 or 4 inches more width than the double-ender, has more stability.

The 19-foot canoe has not been used on most streams. It's more expensive than the shorter double-ender or the shorter square-stern, and rental places can't afford them. But they hold heavy loads and float high. I've used 19-foot square-sterns on the smallest of streams.

The fiberglass canoes I've seen are not suitable for use on any rocky shallow water, because the fiberglass is easily broken. New plastic canoes seem to be fairly effective, but they won't take the heavy blows aluminum or wood will, and they seem to me less stable than aluminum canoes of the same size.

Aluminum johnboats began appearing in the 1950's. Many companies make aluminum boats today, and many are very stable and efficient craft. Aluminum johnboats are best in lengths of 15- to 17-feet. Shorter lengths give less stability, so I recommend the 17-foot length. Heavy-gauge aluminum is an absolute necessity. Boats made of light aluminum are tippy and easily punctured.

Some of the best aluminum johnboats I've seen were made by the Lowe-Line Company in Lebanon, Missouri. This company is an outgrowth of the Richline Company, which styled its early johnboats after the wooden boats built in the Ozarks. Richline representatives visited my grandfather in the early 1950's, and he gave them permission to measure his boats and use those dimensions. Lowe-Line uses .051 gauge aluminum in their boat, a 17-footer, painted a drab green, which should be an absolute necessity as far as I'm concerned, with all aluminum craft.

Lowe-Line makes aluminum boats that have a rake at both ends and are tapered at both ends. This is a tremendous advantage over straight-sided boats without any rake. Boats without a rake are harder to handle, since water piles up against the stern or bow, and the boat doesn't glide easily over the water.

As I write, Lowe-Line sells 17-foot aluminum johnboats for $400–$450. These are the best aluminum johnboats I've found for the price, though these prices—like others—will surely increase. The boats travel very well, handle easily, and are stable with exceptionally heavy loads. Three people can float and fish from a 17-foot aluminum johnboat quite easily in small streams. For 2 fishermen and a good load, the 17-foot boat is easy to handle. It weighs 110 pounds, with 14-inch sides and a 33-inch width.

When aluminum boats are built so much like the original wooden johnboats, they are extremely good river craft. In choosing a boat for floating, the prospective buyer must decide for himself which craft offers the advantages he needs for the type of floating he will be doing. While it's true that wooden johnboats are a great deal cheaper, not everyone can build one. He must also consider that a $400 craft that may last 20 years may be a better buy than a $50 boat that will last about 10 years depending on how it is used.

I would recommend that serious floaters, especially those carrying equipment in all seasons, choose the wooden or aluminum johnboat or the 19-foot square-stern aluminum canoe.

When a floater has become very proficient with a paddle, he will find that a well-built 15-foot wooden boat is easy to handle in most streams and tends to hold course better than other boats. But a wooden johnboat usually is not the best choice for a beginner. You shouldn't try to build and use one until you've at least gained some experience in aluminum johnboats or canoes.

A johnboat is valuable to you if you spend several days at a time on the river with large loads or expensive equipment. If you're a serious river fisherman, if you're interested in gigging or trot-lining, if you wish to hunt or photograph from a boat, the johnboat will be useful to you. If you're interested in traveling in a hurry or doing summertime sight-seeing with a light load, you'd be better off with your choice of canoe.

Chapter 5

Fundamentals of Paddling Your River Craft

I learned long ago that you can't teach people much about how to paddle a boat or canoe. You can show them the fundamental strokes, but then they must learn them through practice and experience.

Beginning floaters often get carried away with the exhilaration of the trip and make costly mental errors. For example, when they approach a shoal or rapids in which a tree or rock presents an obstacle they are likely to forget that they must begin to maneuver around the obstacle even before they enter the shoal. When they wait too long, they're in trouble. That's when the life vests are important. Floating cushions can be carried away by the current and aren't of much help in a river.

When a boat or canoe capsizes in swift water, it is usually because it hits something broadside, tips, and then fills with water. The craft is pinned to (and often wrapped around) the obstacle by the force of the current.

If you start to tip over in such a situation, do everything in your power to avoid being pinned between the boat and the obstacle. The current can be strong enough to keep you there. In these circumstances, your safest move is to exit from the craft on the upstream side.

In calm water, any boat or canoe with proper flotation will float when overturned or filled. In such a case, it is wise to stay with the craft and get it to shore. But in a current where trees and rocks are prevalent, it is best to stay away from the boat or canoe, or at least try to stay upstream from it.

Current is relentless. It stops for nothing or nobody. As it forces a craft under, it can wrap an aluminum hull around the obstacle like a piece of foil. A floater who gets between a boat or canoe and an obstacle is in extreme danger. He can be pinned, a leg or arm can be crushed, and he can even be pulled under.

The wide, deep, quiet eddies of a river are of little threat to a floater. Trouble comes on fast shoals or stretches of curving rapids where you must avoid obstacles. The biggest problems in my region are logs or leaning trees jutting out from the bank at, or just above, the surface.

When you can't go over or under such an obstacle, you're in trouble. A fallen or leaning tree that goes across the current at a 90-degree angle can even block the entire stream. When you see this situation in time, you portage around it. But when you're confronted with such a situation on a sharp bend without warning, your only recourse is to try to backpaddle to slack water.

Of less danger to the floater are midstream obstacles such as large rocks or groups of small willows. Sometimes in high water a stream will split around clumps of trees or even a small island. I determine the best course by picking the side with the greatest flow, but that's not a foolproof method. If both sides look dangerous, it's best to stop and check them out from the bank.

Very often swift-water shoals make a sharp bend. You can't see what you're going into. It's usually wise to check these out on foot from the bank before floating through.

When you enter a bend in swift water, stay to the inside of the curve. Slack water usually occurs on the inside of such bends, and it's easier to get to the inside bank if you meet an obstacle. Periods of high water usually stack logs and other obstacles against the outside edge of a bend. The inside course will normally help you escape them.

Where shoals bend, your ears can often be of help. If you hear a roar around the bend, there may be a rapid fall or drop, or it may be the sound of water piling against a rock or log. Don't proceed till you check out the situation.

In swift water, it's important to keep your craft straight. When

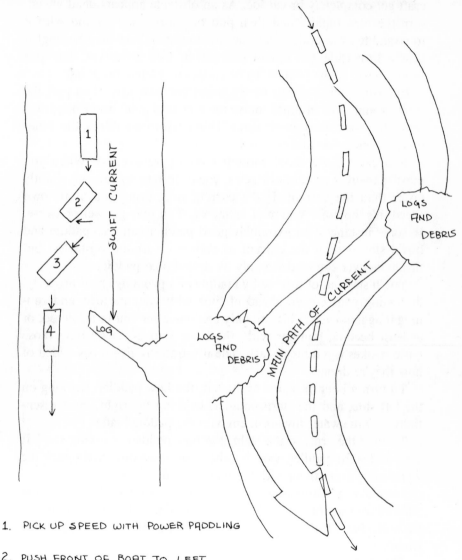

1. PICK UP SPEED WITH POWER PADDLING

2. PUSH FRONT OF BOAT TO LEFT

3. APPLY POWER TO MOVE TOWARDS BANK

4. PULL BACK OF BOAT AROUND TO
   STRAIGHTEN.

it hits an obstacle head-on, you're in trouble, but when it hits an obstacle broadside, you're sunk.

When entering a swift and treacherous shoal, never let your craft get completely broadside. As an obstacle appears dead ahead, turn the bow rapidly and then pull the stern back around with it to straighten the craft. (See the illustration.) You may be angled nearly broadside for a few seconds in this maneuver, but you should never allow yourself to be swept completely broadside.

Entering such a shoal, worry about the bow first, then pull the stern around. For instance, move the bow into quiet water first, then move the stern into quiet water. Don't try to do things the other way around. (See illustration.)

You can't run a shoal without some aggressiveness. When you must maneuver around obstacles, you'll do best by moving slightly faster than the current. If the current is carrying you at its own speed, it's the boss. You're at its mercy. You may get wet or worse. In some instances, an extremely good paddler can backpaddle and travel slower than the current to maneuver around obstacles, but this maneuver can be done only by skilled boat paddlers.

You'll stay out of trouble by reading an upcoming shoal properly, discussing your course ahead of time with your partner, and running it aggressively. This can only be done after you've mastered, or at least become familiar with, the basic strokes. Describing those basic strokes is a difficult task. The illustrations give a basic idea of how they're done.

To turn a boat or canoe to the left, the bow paddler, working on the left side, and the stern paddler, working the right, must essentially *pull* the water toward them with the paddle blade.

To turn the craft to the right, the bow paddler, working the left side, and stern paddler, working the right, must essentially *push* the water away from them with the paddle blade.

To make a johnboat or canoe travel a straight line, the bow paddler uses a straight stroke and the stern paddler uses a J stroke, as shown here. If the sternman is the only paddler, he uses the same stroke.

The J stroke (exaggerated in the illustration) enables you to paddle in a straight line. The first half of the stroke gives you the power necessary to push the boat forward. However, with most people, that portion of the stroke (if you paddle on the right side) will turn the boat slightly to the left. The last half of the stroke, in

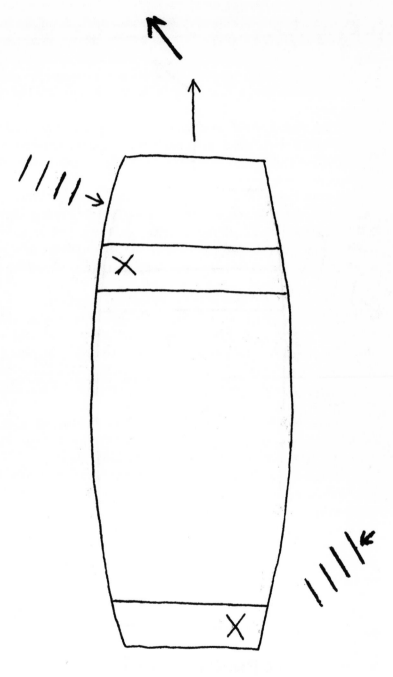

TURNING LEFT

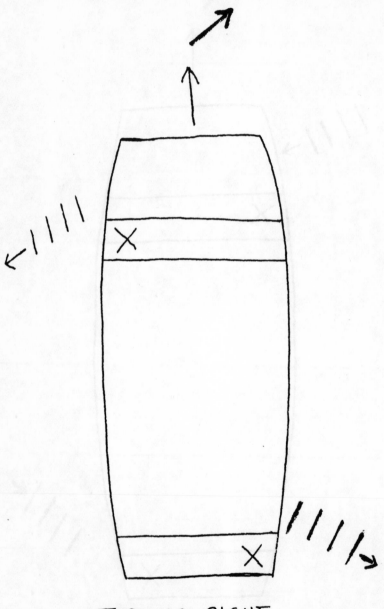

TURNING RIGHT

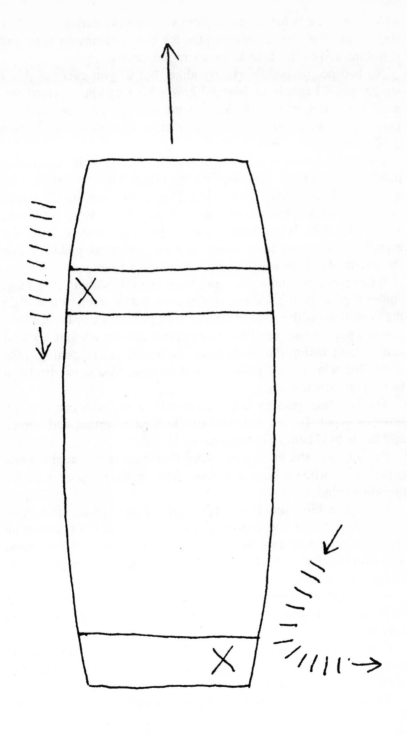

J STROKE

which the blade is turned away from you and the paddle is slightly rotated in your hand, compensates for the tendency to turn and therefore makes the boat keep a straight course.

No two people paddle exactly alike, but as you exercise this J stroke, you'll begin to understand how a boat can be powered forward in a straight line. Paddlers who switch sides constantly to make the craft go straight aren't efficient enough to be floating difficult waters.

I often see canoeists traveling down the river in a zig-zag course, paddling first on one side, then on the other. These people are inexperienced and asking for trouble. They underestimate the power of the current and can't maneuver well enough to avoid problems. Their difficulties begin when they are too impatient to learn the essentials before tackling a stream. Inexperienced paddlers lose thousands of dollars worth of equipment each year.

When you can handle your craft from one side without switching, you're a good boat paddler. You're even better when you can do the same thing with a load, a nonpaddling passenger, or both. When you can paddle your craft for long periods of time without a sound and without taking the blade from the water, you're getting quite good. But being a good paddler is not enough. You must also learn to read the stream.

The best boat paddler is not necessarily a guy who can run any shoal or rapid. It's the guy who can look at a certain bad stretch and know he'd better portage around it.

Reading the stream is something that cannot be taught. Only experience—with perhaps some help from instinct—gives a floater this knowledge.

In approaching shoals or rapids, the floater must often look ahead and choose the proper course. In scanning an upcoming shoal, he should be able to discern the deeper water, the strongest part of a current, and whirlpools. He also needs to recognize submerged logs and rocks, which may be hard to detect.

An important aspect of floating is the paddles you use. Have 3 or 4 on each trip, with the extra on top of any load and within easy reach.

Cheap paddles cause a lot of capsized craft. Buy good strong paddles. Next best to the sassafras paddles the old-time guides once made and used are probably today's laminated ones.

There is no ironclad rule about paddle lengths, but usually you'll do best with one that reaches from the ground to just beneath your chin when you're standing. If you like a shorter paddle, try one that comes to your armpit. I use the shorter paddles only when photographing wildlife or hunting. The shorter length allows me to minimize arm movements, which might show over the blind that I attach to the front of my boat.

Chapter 6

How to Have a Successful Float Trip

If you're a beginner to floating, start out easy. Take your johnboat to a quiet stretch of water and practice until you get the hang of things. While you're learning, be sure to wear that personal flotation device and clothes that you don't mind getting soaked. In fact, don't take anything with you that you can't afford to get wet.

Get accustomed to paddling your craft in quiet water. Learn how to make it turn quickly, how to back it up, and how to go forward in a straight line. You're beginning to learn the fundamentals when you have developed the ability to paddle in a straight course from one side of the boat, without switching. Until you learn that basic skill, you shouldn't be thinking of loading a boat or canoe and making a long trip.

As you learn to handle your boat better, make short trips with little or no load down streams that aren't difficult. Don't go out and tackle a stretch of white water somewhere that you aren't ready for. First learn to run some easy shoals and straight chutes of swift water. Take short empty trips until you feel comfortable in your boat and it responds quickly the way you want it to.

I've seen people learn to master a johnboat or canoe in a matter of days, but I've observed others who never learned to paddle proficiently. For most people, 2 or 3 short trips down an average stream will go a long way toward teaching proper handling.

Another caution: when you're learning, stay away from high waters. Tackle streams that are normal, even a little low. Don't go to the swift, bankful streams till later.

And no matter how skillful you become, there are some shoals

70

and rapids that you just can't run. Lots of times I pull around such shoals. Some, I know I can't run. Others, I may not be able to run. I don't take stupid chances with my life and with equipment that is worth a lot to me.

Looking at a shoal or swift water and knowing whether you can run it safely or not comes only with lots of experience. Some of our heavily floated streams have places that no one can navigate.

When you're paddling well, handling your boat proficiently, and beginning to feel comfortable in it, you may begin to take longer trips and carry more equipment. I believe in personal flotation devices (PFD's). Anyone in your boat who's unable to swim well should always be wearing one. I firmly believe that children, even if they can swim well, should have a flotation device on while they are floating. Many times I don't wear one because I feel it limits my movements, and I have become a good swimmer.

When I was growing up on a river, we never had PFD's. I seldom wear one, because of my confidence in myself and the knowledge I have of the rivers I float. Most of these rivers are small and offer little threat to an experienced floater. But where there is danger—on a swollen stream or on a large, swift stream—I usually wear one. Only experience allows a person to know which water represents a threat and which doesn't. If you don't have that experience, be safe and wear your PFD.

Wooden johnboats (because of natural buoyancy) and most aluminum boats and canoes (because of factor-installed flotation) won't sink in calm water. But if any of these craft lodge against an object in swift water, they will tip, fill with water, and sometimes be forced down by the current.

This is one reason I don't recommend tieing anything in the boat. Sleeping bags, clothing, and personal effects that will float should be sealed in two thicknesses of plastic bags used for lining garbage cans. This arrangement will keep them dry, even if they go into the river.

If you have something valuable with you that will sink, you might want to try a method I've seen used. Camera equipment should be kept in a waterproof army ammo box. This will sink, but 10 or 12 feet of cord with one end tied to the handle and the other fastened to a small floating piece of styrofoam will help you recover it, should you turn over. The cord-and-buoy idea is good for campstoves, lanterns, and other gear that will sink.

In ammo boxes you might wish to carry matches and a small radio, as well as topographic maps. I hate the noise of a radio on a float trip. But in the spring I carry a small one to check severe-weather warnings.

The topographic map is one of the most valuable things you can take on a river. It helps you keep track of how much river you're covering each hour and how much you need to cover before arriving at a take-out point. Your topo map shows the closest roads and farm houses or settlements (handy in case of emergency). The map showing some rivers will show sheer bluffs or caves that can provide protection from high winds or heavy rains.

By examining your topo map closely, you may detect areas of extreme drop. The rate of fall can be calculated, helping you to predict the swiftest water or falls. If I don't know the river I'm floating, a topographic map is as important to me as a spare paddle.

As time goes on, you'll become efficient with a paddle. Only then should you consider serious fishing, hunting, or overnight floating.

Preparing for an overnight float trip is important. Faulty preparation can lead to misery on trips of a few days.

I use a checklist to help me prepare. The checklist for a 3- or 4-day spring fishing trip for 2 men might look like this:

—First Ammo Box: Camera and lenses
—Second Ammo Box: Matches
                        Vial of carbide (for starting fires
                           in rain)
                        Roll of nylon cord—300 lb. test
                        First-aid kit—snake-bite kit
                        Heavy hunting knife
                        Pen and note pad
                        Maps
                        Transistor radio (for weather
                           warnings)
                        Extra mantles for lantern
                        Handful of 3-inch nails
—Container with drinking water—1–3 gallons
—Small belt axe
—Cook set
—Extra skillet

—2-man tent, lightweight
—Sleeping bags in double garbage-can plastic liners
—Extra clothing in double garbage-can plastic liners:
  This bundle should include personal effects such as
  toothbrush, razor, and so on, several pairs of dry socks
  and underwear, and a pair of hiking boots or shoes.
—Coleman stove, and or campfire grill
—Coleman lantern and one gallon of fuel
—Pair of strong flashlights
—Ultralight fishing tackle and small tackle box
—Pair of folding camp stools
—Two plywood rectangles, 2 × 3 up to 4 × 3 (used for
  camp tables)
—Three or four paddles
—Two 8 × 10 sheets of heavy gauge plastic
—Two small plastic buckets

The following are suggestions for groceries. Naturally, I don't
mean to suggest you take all of this on one trip.

—Metal cooler with ice: Butter
                        Eggs
                        Quarts or pints of milk
                        Sausage
                        Cheese and lunchmeats
                        Hamburger
                        Sandwich spread
                        Lettuce
                        Tomatoes
                        Soft drinks
—Styrofoam dry cooler: Small roll of paper towels
                        Aluminum foil
                        Box of garbage-can plastic
                          liners (use for trash)
                        Pot holder
                        Egg turner and fish fork
                        Can opener and silverware
                        Soap pads—small container of
                          dish-washing soap

Bar of hand soap
Bread or crackers
Coffee, salt, pepper, sugar in
　　small containers
Canned goods (beans, stew,
　　　　　　　potatoes, chili,
　　　　　　　peaches, pears,
　　　　　　　etc.)
Cooking oil
Raw potatoes
Apples, oranges, and bananas
Cookies
Corn meal or flour
Instant packets (hot chocolate,
　　　　　　　oatmeal, pota-
　　　　　　　toes, etc.)

Food is a matter of choice of course, but there are some things that make grocery storage easier. For instance, rather than packing a couple dozen eggs, subject to breaking, you can crack the shells and empty raw eggs into a small Tupperware juice container with a pour hole. The eggs, when needed, will pour out one at a time without breaking. They're easier to use in this form and take up half the space of eggs in shells.

I use 2 coolers, 1 Coleman metal cooler, the other a lighter styrofoam cooler. In the styrofoam box I store nonperishable goods, and food that needn't be on ice. In the metal cooler, I store perishable food. On float trips, it's unwise to take cubed or crushed ice. Blocks of ice last much longer. You can make your own by freezing water in 3 or 4 1-inch gallon milk cartons. In very hot weather, it's best to buy 1 large block.

It's not practical to take along food that occupies lots of space and really doesn't provide much benefit. Marshmallows and potato chips fall into this category. Cases of beverages are nice to have on hot trips in midsummer, but they take up a great deal of space and may not be worth carrying. Ice-tea mix is sometimes preferred over large quantities of soda.

Midday meals on the river are usually light: sandwiches, fruit, and cookies. Breakfasts are also usually simple. But evening meals on the river may be more complicated. Canned stew and chili make

74

good easy hot meals and take up little space. Some floaters like to go all out and have steak and salad. Others like hamburgers and beans.

I'm partial to fresh fish on float trips. It's something you can catch along the way, and all that's necessary for a good meal is some luck, corn meal, and cooking oil. However, it's good to have something to fall back on, just in case the fish aren't hitting.

Camps on the river are more comfortable at mealtime if you have a small table or 2. This is why I carry a couple of plywood rectangles with me. With a hole in each corner of the plywood, all I have to do is cut 4 legs from dead driftwood and nail the plywood top to them. When I'm floating, the legs are removed, and the plywood rests on those wooden legs, just an inch or so off the bottom. This arrangement keeps my gear off the boat floor and dry.

I don't believe I've ever floated a river anywhere, in a johnboat or any other craft, without getting some water in the boat before the end of the trip. Water runs off the blade of a paddle when you lay it down to fish for a moment, and water splashes in on the rough shoals. In winter, moisture can condense inside an aluminum boat or canoe.

On many streams, it's necessary to do quite a bit of wading. You may want to fish a shoal or stretch of swift water by wading before you float through it. Or you may have to pull around an impassable stretch of water.

If you float without getting a drop of water in a boat, you've really done something. Chances are you won't be that fortunate. I recommend that you take steps to keep articles you want to keep dry off the floor of the boat.

From fall through early summer, a floater must wear hip boots or waders. But in the summer, tennis shoes (or other wading shoes with good gripping soft soles) are the ticket. Since many stream bottoms are solid rock or are made up of large rocks, wading can be tricky. Wet rock can be slicker than ice.

Whatever the season, be sure to include heavier clothing for nights on the river. Even in summer, nighttime on a stream can become cool.

When you prepare for a float trip of any length, about the wisest thing you can do is take the time to pack your boat properly. The way seating is arranged in boats and canoes, the weight of 2 passengers isn't distributed equally in front and back. Normally, the front of the craft sets up just a little, with weight just slightly heavier toward the stern. This is as it should be, but don't get too much weight toward the back. Passengers will shift the balance even more, toward the rear, so try to load equipment and cargo around the center of your boat. If anything, load these things a bit heavier toward the front.

Heavy items should go as low in the boat as possible, with lighter gear on top. It doesn't take much experience to load a boat properly. When you have it completely loaded, your cargo may rise 6 to 8 inches above the boat or canoe sides. It shouldn't rise higher than that if you expect to float safely.

When your craft is loaded, it's not a bad idea to cover the load with a tarpaulin or a sheet of heavy gauge plastic. I like the plastic because its lighter. When it covers your gear and is tucked in on all sides, you can float in a heavy rain without much worry.

At night, a pair of these plastic sheets can come in handy. One protects my camp equipment in case of rain, and I use the other to cover the small lightweight nylon tent. These small 2-man tents are convenient for floating, but in heavy rains they leak a little—especially if you touch the sides at one place or another. So when rain threatens, use that second sheet of plastic to cover the tent, and keep you dry inside.

A heavily loaded boat or canoe is, as you'd expect, harder for you and your partner to control and slower to respond than is an empty craft. Be a little more cautious. A shoal or rough stretch of water that you can easily navigate with an empty boat may become more of a problem when you're carrying equipment. To make up for the extra weight, decide as early as possible about course changes you want to take.

By contrast, a lone traveler finds it hard to navigate without some balancing weight. When I float alone, I put a couple or 3 heavy rocks in the left front of my boat to level it when I'm sitting to the right in the stern.

Many years ago, people in the Ozarks where I grew up would have laughed at the idea of carrying drinking water on a float trip. But the use of agricultural chemicals today is so extensive that even much spring water is contaminated. Stream water, no matter how pure it looks, shouldn't be used in preparing food or drinking water. If it's boiled, perhaps there's little danger in using stream water for coffee or washing dishes, but even the clearest, cleanest looking water can be impure. Spring water can be impure, and it can have harsh effects even if it's pure.

Many a time it has happened that canoeists from large cities in other regions get ill in the Ozarks from drinking spring water known to be pure. Such spring water, often high in mineral content, can be so different from what a person is accustomed to that it causes minor stomach problems and diarrhea.

If you run out of water, boil stream water each night. Let it cool overnight for use the following day.

By wisely choosing your supplies and supplementing them with fish and wild meat in season, you can float for many days at a time without having to replenish your supplies. For most people, 5 to 10 days of floating is a real experience.

The key to successful floating, whether for one day or several, is good planning and preparation. With a topographic map, you can plan the distance you'll float each day and generally find camp sites that will most suit you. In spring and summer, for instance, severe storms in my part of the nation can develop in a matter of hours. Bluffs that face east or north can sometimes provide shallow shelters.

A bad storm on the river is rough to endure. High winds or tornadoes aren't the only danger. Lightning and hail can be dangerous, too. If you seek shelter from hail beneath a tree, you may be in danger from lightning. In an aluminum craft of any kind, lightning is something to be concerned about.

It's customary in the Midwest to camp on gravel or sand bars. If a storm is imminent, seek higher ground. Rivers can rise several feet in a matter of hours. I know of many occasions when floaters have lost all their gear to a rising river. Occasionally someone will camp on a gravel bar on the river and ignore low ground or a dry channel behind them. A 4- or 5-foot rise in the river may not only take away the boat or canoe that was left pulled up to the gravel bar but may also make an island of the camp site by changing the low ground behind it into a flowing channel.

Be sure when you make camp that you're far enough away from the water to withstand a rise in the river and to give yourself enough time to get your equipment out. And be sure there's high ground behind you, so you don't get surrounded and trapped.

In the heat of summer, it's nice to camp on sand and gravel bars. But in the fall, winter, or early spring, you might be more comfortable a little further away from the river in a clean wooded area or in a small grassy meadow. Dampness is less of a problem when you're slightly away from the river.

When you're floating, it's a good idea to stop and pitch camp an hour or so before dusk. This schedule gives you time to check out the area, gather firewood, and so on. If you expect a storm, find a bluff shelter if possible, or perhaps a high bank that can protect a tent from the wind. Because of lightning, stay away from trees and fences. And don't crawl under an aluminum craft for shelter. As I mentioned before, a small transistor radio is valuable during stormy weather for floaters who wish to receive area weather warnings.

A tent is poor shelter in a severe storm, but it can be made passable if bluff shelters aren't available. Be sure your tent is well staked and is set up in an area that best protects it from lightning, rising water, and winds.

Don't try to float through a severe storm. Find the best protection you can and sit it out. And if a river rises drastically, don't float while it's flooded. You're best off to stow the equipment you can't carry, and walk out, returning later for the gear.

Some floaters, after enduring a storm on the river, choose never to make another float. It's a humbling experience, but something all men should experience. As you sit in a tent that's suddenly far too flimsy, listening to lightning crackle about you, followed by deafening roars of thunder and tree limbs cracking with the wind, you realize what a powerless insignificant creature man can be.

Chapter 7

The Life of an Ozark River Guide

I learned to paddle a johnboat when I was 11 years old. There was a big eddy about 2 or 3 miles from our house called the Ginseng eddy, and above it was the Sweet Potato eddy. In these 2 big holes lurked a smallmouth bass such as no one had ever seen. My intentions were to catch that lunker smallmouth, which I figured might have gone over the 6-pound mark.

Now it would have been easier to do that if I hadn't had to hold down a pretty important job in nearby Houston. That year, Dad had bought the local pool hall. It was a country pool hall, a hangout for the hunters and fishermen of the area and for the old-timers who had known the river even before my dad was born.

During the day, my grandfather McNew ran the place. I arose at daylight 6 days a week, pedaled my bike into town to the pool hall on Main Street, and helped my grandpa clean up before opening. That summer I sat wide-eyed and open-mouthed, listening to a collection of 60- and 70-year-old men recall the good old days, right there on the bench with 3 huge fish mounted on the wall, and a row of spittoons beneath them.

I was close to Grandpa McNew. He was a sage of man, with the wisdom of countless aging men who have seen it all, and could well advise us of a better course if younger men would only listen.

My other grandfather, Grandpa Dablemont, and my father taught me to fish and hunt. Grandpa Dablemont made me realize there was much to be learned that books couldn't teach. Grandpa McNew taught me there was much to be learned from everything, including books. Not only that, he taught me how to shoot pool, how to snooker the other fellow, play the leave, and put English on the ball.

For 6 years I worked in the old pool hall, and learned to idolize a handful of old men who didn't mind telling stories to a kid. Grandpa let me rack tables and collect money. And when he stepped out for lunch or some other reason, I got to run the place. I usually worked part of each weekday during the summers. And in the winter, I worked in the pool hall after school, sometimes until closing time, sometimes just a couple of hours.

But come 3 o'clock, I was on my bicycle and gone. I'd stop by home for my shotgun or rod and reel. With one or the other tied across the handle bars, I'd head for the river to hunt squirrels or fish for that big smallmouth.

The old gravel road had some hills in it, but at the end of it was Myrtle Kelly's farm. Mrs. Kelly was a kindly lady who owned the prettiest place on the river. She was a widow, but in years gone by she and her husband had fished with Grandpa Dablemont all over the Ozarks. She had one of Grandpa's old johnboats fastened to a tree, chained and locked, and all I had to do was ask her for the key. Sometimes she'd go along, and we'd dig a can of night crawlers, or set a minnow trap, and stillfish at the upper end of the Sweet 'tater eddy. Her nephew from Oklahoma spent some time with her, and he and I fished together on occasion.

But much of the time, I fished alone, each evening until dusk, trying to hook that big one.

Seems like once or twice a week I'd hook that big bass, but I'd never get to see him. Every time I'd hook a big turtle, or catfish or log, or rock, it was that big bass until proven otherwise.

Then every morning at the pool hall I'd sit in the middle of the bench and tell Ol' Bill, and Ol' Jim, and Ol' Jess, and General, and Churchill, and Grandpa McNew how close I'd come to haulin' that big smallmouth in by the gills.

They'd all listen, and glance at one another from time to time, winkin' and grinnin', which used to make me madder'n hell.

By the end of the first summer, I'd learned to handle the johnboat reasonably well, though I lacked the strength to really be good with a paddle. I did my first guiding for my dad and grandpa and uncles and cousins that summer and fall. A couple of local fishermen who were good friends of my grandfather would come by and pick me up on Saturday afternoons and have me paddle for them while they fished.

I was the only guide on the Big Piney you could get for 50¢. And though I never told anyone, I'd have paddled all day for nothing if they'd just listened without grinning to how close I'd come to catching that smallmouth.

The following summer, Grandpa Dablemont and I did a lot of trotlining, and I did more guiding on weekends. We caught the big bass that year on a trotline, and turned it loose. The men at the pool hall began to dread seeing me coming.

When I was 13, I got my first guide's license so I could get paid legally and better for my services. My business was mostly people from the city who'd floated with my dad and uncles when they were younger.

Before my first trip as a licensed guide, my dad gave me some advice. "Just paddle the boat, son," he said. "Don't give advice on fishin'."

Early that morning, my client cast a small spinner toward the bank, in shallow water with a gravel bottom and not a rock or log within 50 yards.

"You won't catch anything there," I told him. "Too shallow, and not enough cover."

Just as I finished, a fat half-pound goggle-eye grabbed the lure. The fisherman hauled him in. I didn't say much the rest of the day.

Grandpa later told me about a wise old guide who practically never talked. One day he was particularly quiet and hadn't said a word all morning. Just before the lunch stop, his client hooked the old guide's hat on the back cast and flung it into the river. The old guide let loose with a long string of cuss words, and the fisherman was a little relieved.

"Why is it," he asked, "that you haven't said a thing all morning until just now?"

"Wal," the old-timer said as he shifted his tobacco in his cheek and retrieved his dripping hat, "up to now you was a-doin' all right."

Grandpa had become a guide when he was in his teens, but in that day everyone wanted to hunt. Fishing wasn't something you needed a guide for. Most fishing in the Midwest was done with natural bait. In the East and North, fly fishing was fairly popular. But way back then, there wasn't much of what we know as fishing today, because there weren't any reels you could cast with. The advent of good casting reels made possible the popularity of float-fishing with artificial lures, and float-fishing focused attention on the free-flowing streams of the Midwest.

The process took a while because, after World War I, fishing lures were expensive. Flies, by contrast, were simple to make and economical. Wooden lures that cost $1 to $1.75 were high in that day and time. So fly fishing remained the popular way of sport fishing in our area until after World War II. Float-fishing guides and their johnboats provided excellent services for fly fishermen who sought smallmouth, largemouth, Kentucky and rock bass, as well as green sunfish and other species of panfish.

The improvement of casting reels did a lot for the fellow who made his living with a johnboat and paddle. Casting reels and heavier lures allowed rivermen to turn from commercial fishing (which was becoming complicated by new game laws) to teaching and helping others catch fish.

The guide's main job was to paddle the boat, maneuvering it into the best fishing positions and holding it in swift water where smallmouths lurked. He kept the fisherman the right distance from the bank, and he retrieved lures that got hung up beneath the surface. He also had to know the best fishing lures and where the fish were in different seasons.

On overnight trips, the guide prepared the meals, collected firewood, and cleaned the fish. Few of them complained about anything. Guiding was the work most of them were meant for. It was the most enjoyable thing they did. It brought together two different ways of life: the well-to-do city sportsman and the backwoods philosopher who found happiness in simple things.

The guide was a naturalist, an interpreter of the river and its life. There was no thrill like helping someone else enjoy the outdoors solely because of your ability. A guide took pride in that. And through my own experiences, I know that most guides enjoyed seeing a client catch a fish more than they themselves enjoyed catching one. That was the real test of competence. If you could take inexperienced fishermen and help them enjoy a successful trip, there was no question of your own fishing ability.

Float fishermen came from every walk of life, and strong friendships grew between the guides and fishermen he worked for. There were people that a guide hated to see leave, and he might look forward to their return as much as to a visit from relatives. And in turn, sportsmen and their families sometimes planned their vacations around a visit to one area where their favorite guide would set aside all other work to cater to them. Quite often, wealthy sportsmen would leave elaborate and expensive homes in the city and bring a son to spend a week in a small cabin on a Midwestern river with an old river guide.

My uncle, Norten Dablemont, from Rogers, Arkansas, who is semiretired but still guiding on a limited scale in northwest Arkansas, began guiding in the 1930's in southern Missouri. He was just a boy at the time. After he returned from World War II, he began guiding for a St. Louis fisherman named Carl Emmick.

Emmick was a wealthy man without a family, and he immediately took to Norten, providing him with new equipment, teaching him to use casting reels and artificial lures.

Of the friendship, Norten told me, "He was like an old lady as he grew older, and I took care of him. When I guided for Mr. Emmick, he didn't even tie his own lures, as his vision become poor in old age. He'd pick me up in southern Missouri, and we'd fish all over the country. He took care of all expenses and equipment; I did all the work. But despite the fact that he paid me well for my services, he was more than a client. He was a friend, like a father to me. He taught me more about life than anyone else. We usually made 2 or 3 trips a month and at least 1 every month. Each trip would last 3 or 4 days."

Emmick and my uncle fished together from 1947 to 1972, when the old man died at the age of 80. He continued to fish right up to the month of his death. Despite his age and weakness, he could enjoy fishing because he had the best guide he could find.

There wasn't always such friendship developing between a sportsman and guide. Some of the fishermen retreating from the city didn't want to get away from it "all." They'd bring along enough booze to last a month. Those kind of people were a problem. They often became intoxicated before the trip was half finished. In such a condition, they were in danger, and a threat to the safety of the guide.

A drunk, whipping around a big lure with treble hooks on it, could inflict some painful damage, and even cost someone an eye. And a client in that shape might fall in and drown before the guide could get to him.

So most guides refused to take anyone who wanted to mix drinking and fishing. One old-timer said, "I figger a man who has to have likker when he's fishin' ain't gonna enjoy the river much. If'n he wants to drink, he can stay home an' drink. If'n he wants to fish, he don't need the stuff."

In their day as river guides, Grandpa and his 4 sons didn't take anyone on a float trip who drank. A few cans of beer were all right, but when a guy broke out a bottle or hauled in a cooler completely filled with beer, he had to look elsewhere for a guide.

Every now and then somebody would sneak a flask along in a coat pocket. My dad recalls a fellow who floated with him in early spring many years ago. Dad was only 15. And though a grown man could refuse to paddle for someone who was drinking, a boy couldn't exert much authority.

When he asked the fisherman to put away the bottle, Dad was told he was to paddle the boat and keep his mouth shut. By noon, the fisherman was very drunk. His casts were going everywhere. Finally, he decided to stand on the front seat so he could fish better. This maneuver made the boat difficult to handle. Over Dad's objections, the very inebriated angler insisted he wouldn't fall out, declaring himself an expert on balance.

Dad eyed a shoal ahead, only a couple of feet deep, with a gentle current and a snag just below the surface. Picking up speed, he hit the snag just as his client took another drink.

Dad recalls the results with a grin. The bottle was lost, and the "expert on balance" was sobered considerably by the early-spring water temperature.

Dad's brother Vaughn found another way to discourage drinking. Like all guides, he hated to get a lure out of the branches every 5 minutes. When a man was drinking, of course, his casts were never short.

Vaughn was a pistol enthusiast, and he had a small .22 revolver he took along on most of his trips. One day he had a client who was drinking heavily and couldn't be persuaded to quit. After retrieving lures from bushes along the bank for an hour or so, Vaughn got the opportunity he was looking for.

The fisherman lofted the lure into a tree limb just barely in reach. He suggested that his guide stand on the seat and retrieve it, but Vaughn had a better idea: he would shoot the limb in two. He took careful aim and emptied the pistol, the plug splintering with a couple of straying (or well placed) bullets.

With a shrug of his shoulders, Vaughn holstered the pistol and suggested his client find another lure. The fisherman sobered up enough to be more careful with his casts.

As times changed, the river guide became a rarity as did the johnboat that was his constant companion. Aluminum canoes and boats helped bring about the change, as sport fishermen began to acquire their own craft and float on their own.

Besides, the rivermen who loved the life of a guide became too old, and their sons moved away to work in the cities where the lights were bright and money easier to come by.

Oh, there are still guides to be found, but they aren't the fellows in flannel shirts who eased the johnboat along a quiet river with a sassafras paddle.

In Arkansas today, one of the state's premier smallmouth streams attracts guides from a nearby reservoir with 20-foot fiberglass john-boats and motors. The river isn't big enough for the invasion. The motors produce wakes that erode the banks, and the floaters usually miss the best the stream has to offer. A stringer of fish is the sign that indicates success, and a boat paddle is used only when the motor goes out or the shoals are too shallow.

As in most waters today, float-fishing streams have received con-siderable pressure. The fishing isn't the way it once was when big smallmouths lurked beneath every fallen log or submerged stump. The heyday of float-fishing was the day of the wooden johnboat, the sassafras paddle, and the leather-faced guide who wouldn't have traded places with a king.

Index

87